ANIMALS OF THE
ARCTIC

by Elizabeth Crane

Scott Foresman
is an imprint of

PEARSON

Glenview, Illinois • Boston, Massachusetts • Chandler, Arizona
Upper Saddle River, New Jersey

Photo locators denoted as follows: Top (T), Center (C), Bottom (B), Left (L), Right (R), Background (Bkgd)

Opener: Fritz Polking/Peter Arnold, Inc.; 1 Getty Images; 3 Getty Images; 5 (C) ©DK Images, (B) Getty Images; 6 ©N. Rosing/UNEP/Peter Arnold, Inc.; 8 Getty Images; 10 Getty Images; 11 ©DK Images; 13 Art Wolfe/Getty Images; 15 Getty Images; 16 Fritz Polking/Peter Arnold, Inc.; 19 Getty Images; 20 Getty Images; 22 ©M. A. Chappell/ Animals Animals/Earth Scenes

ISBN 13: 978-0-328-52613-0
ISBN 10:   0-328-52613-4

3 4 5 6 7 8 9 10 V0N4 13 12 11 10

ISBN 13: 978-0-328-52613-0
ISBN 10:   0-328-52613-4

3 4 5 6 7 8 9 10 V0N4 13 12 11 10

ANIMALS OF THE ARCTIC

by Elizabeth Crane

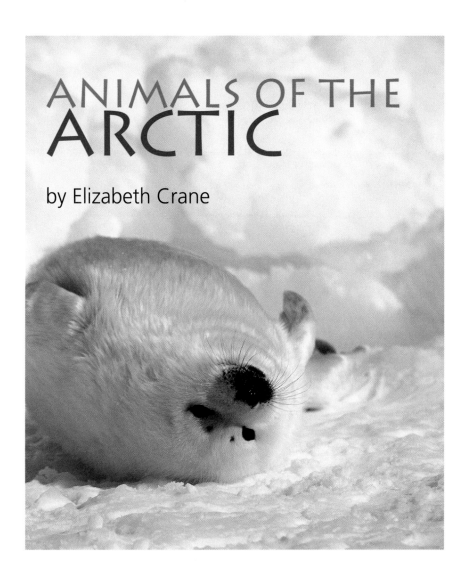

Scott Foresman
is an imprint of

Glenview, Illinois • Boston, Massachusetts • Chandler, Arizona
Upper Saddle River, New Jersey

Every effort has been made to secure permission and provide appropriate credit for photographic material. The publisher deeply regrets any omission and pledges to correct errors called to its attention in subsequent editions.

Unless otherwise acknowledged, all photographs are the property of Scott Foresman, a division of Pearson Education.

Photo locators denoted as follows: Top (T), Center (C), Bottom (B), Left (L), Right (R), Background (Bkgd)

Opener: Fritz Polking/Peter Arnold, Inc.; 1 Getty Images; 3 Getty Images; 5 (C) ©DK Images, (B) Getty Images; 6 ©N. Rosing/UNEP/Peter Arnold, Inc.; 8 Getty Images; 10 Getty Images; 11 ©DK Images; 13 Art Wolfe/Getty Images; 15 Getty Images; 16 Fritz Polking/Peter Arnold, Inc.; 19 Getty Images; 20 Getty Images; 22 ©M. A. Chappell/ Animals Animals/Earth Scenes

ISBN 13: 978-0-328-52613-0
ISBN 10:   0-328-52613-4

Suppose you are taking an **expedition** to a place where it is dark even in the early afternoon. As you stand outside, imagine huge gusts of wind and temperatures that make your ears sting with cold. Imagine a landscape of snow and only a few trees. There are huge sheets of ice floating by in the freezing ocean water. Some of these sheets of ice are several miles across.

It is winter now, but if you were to return during the summer, you would see patches of grass and moss where the snow has melted. Underneath the moss and grass, the soil below the surface remains frozen, even in the summer. You would be on Earth's northernmost piece of land. Welcome to the Arctic!

As you are nearly blown over by the strength of the arctic wind, you have never been more thankful for the warmth of your mittens, snowsuit, and thick down jacket. Your clothing is helping you stay **insulated** from the cold. However, you quickly realize that this clothing alone would not keep you warm enough to survive for long in the Arctic. Without the extra protection of shelter, you wouldn't be able to survive in this harsh winter climate. Luckily, you have a shelter, and you have also brought along the necessary **provisions.**

This is your first time visiting the Arctic, and you are feeling a little lost in all the ice and snow. Luckily for you, you also have a friend who has come along to help. She knows all about the Arctic. She will show you how to survive in such a harsh climate and will be a helpful **navigator** for this adventure!

You wonder what you will see or do here. After all, it looks like a very lonely place. However, your friend assures you that there are many animals here too. You just have to look closely. She promises you that you won't be in **isolation** after all.

The Arctic is made up of the land and ocean north of the Arctic Circle, including parts of Europe, Asia, North America, and Greenland.

As you explore the Arctic landscape during this winter season, think about your surroundings. What does the land look like? What kind of animals might you see? How do you think these animals survive in the snow and ice?

You wonder how they are able to find enough food. How do they keep themselves warm in such freezing temperatures? What special characteristics do these arctic animals have?

You turn to your friend with these questions. Rather than explain it, she decides to show you some of the unique animals that call the Arctic Circle their home.

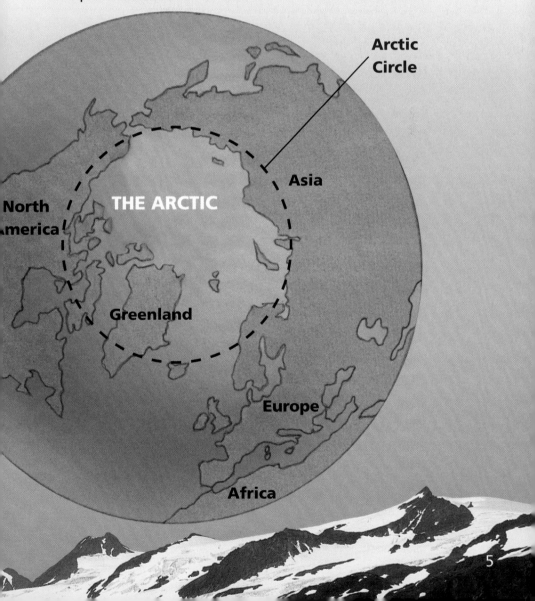

Arctic Circle

Asia

North America

THE ARCTIC

Greenland

Europe

Africa

Along the shore or on the frozen ocean, you may see polar bears. Polar bears are skilled and strong arctic predators. The polar bear's white fur coat makes the animal difficult to see in the snowy and icy arctic landscape.

You may even catch sight of a polar bear swimming in the Arctic Ocean. They are strong swimmers and have been spotted many miles from land or ice packs.

The large polar bear blends into the snowy Arctic landscape.

Polar bears are carnivorous, or meat-eating, mammals. During the winter, they walk on the ice and search for seals. The pads on the underside of a polar bear's paws prevent it from sliding on the slippery surfaces. In the Arctic, the wind gusts are strong and the temperatures are well below freezing, a thick fur coat and layer of blubber insulate the polar bear. Blubber is a layer of fat between their skin and muscles.

Polar bears hunt seals for food. The seals swim under the ocean's thick sheet of winter ice, where the water is very cold. Like other mammals, seals breathe air. They come up for air through large holes in the ice layer called breathing holes.

When polar bears find a breathing hole in the ice, they know that seals are nearby. Very quietly, the polar bear waits for its next meal to come closer. When a seal gets near the breathing hole, the polar bear leaps forward, using its sharp claws to catch the seal and pull it out of the water.

Polar bears are large animals. Males can weigh up to 1,600 pounds. Polar bears have been able to **conquer** the Arctic's harsh environment.

Seals are also carnivorous mammals. They eat mostly fish. They also have a thick coat of blubber, which insulates them against the arctic water. Baby seals, called pups, are born without blubber, but they quickly grow a layer of it to keep warm.

Seals are very good swimmers. They can stay underwater for as long as thirty minutes. When they are swimming, seals find fish for their next meal.

Seals have torpedo-shaped bodies and powerful paddle-like flippers. Their flippers are turned backward, which makes swimming easier. However, the shape of their flippers makes walking on land very difficult. Imagine what it would be like trying to walk with your feet pointing backward! That's what it is like for a seal. For this reason, seals slide on the ice instead.

Seals are part of a larger group of animals called pinnipeds. This means "fin-footed." Seven species of seals live in the Arctic: ringed seals, bearded seals, spotted seals, ribbon seals, hooded seals, grey seals, and harp seals. All seven species share the same predators—polar bears and humans. Seals are hunted for their meat, fur, and blubber.

A seal pup's white fur helps it blend
in with the snow.

The arctic fox is difficult to find, but with enough time and patience, you may be able to see this animal during your arctic adventure. The arctic fox always blends in with its surroundings, because the color of its fur changes with the seasons.

During the longer winter season, its fur is white or silver-gray. As the snow falls, an arctic fox with white fur blends into its environment and is less likely to be seen by wolves and other predators.

During the shorter summer season, however, its fur is brown or dark gray. The snow no longer covers the soil, rocks, and plants. Now, darker fur will blend better into the environment.

The thickness of the arctic fox's fur also changes as the seasons pass. During the winter season, its fur coat is thick to protect it from the cold air. During the summer, the air is warmer, so the fox's coat becomes thinner.

Short rounded ears, a short muzzle, and fur-covered feet also help to protect it from the cold. With smaller ears and a smaller muzzle, less of the fox's skin is exposed to the cold. Fur on the bottoms of its feet allows the fox to walk across the frozen ground without damaging its paws.

During the summer, the arctic fox has a brown or dark gray fur coat.

During the winter, the arctic fox has a white or silver-gray fur coat.

Arctic foxes live in burrows dug into the ground. This protects them from the wind and cold. They are active during the day and will eat whenever food is available.

The arctic fox is skilled at finding food and avoiding its predators. It moves very quickly. This way, it is more likely to escape its predators and to find enough food to live.

Arctic foxes hunt small animals, such as rodents and young birds. Sometimes an arctic fox will follow a polar bear, hoping to eat the bear's leftover food. But it must be careful to stay unnoticed by the larger carnivore. Otherwise, the **destiny** of the arctic fox will be to become the bear's next meal! The camouflage and speed of the arctic fox help it avoid its predators' watchful eyes.

The arctic hare also has white fur to help it stay unseen by its predators. It will travel in groups of its own kind to give it a sense of security while it searches for food. When a hare is threatened, it will stand on its hind legs and hop away as quickly as it can.

Arctic hares live only in open regions, where the wind blows the snow away from the ground. This way, it is easier for them to find food. Hares will eat roots, grasses, berries, and mosses.

The ears of the arctic hare are smaller than those of other hares. This helps prevent the loss of body heat.

Like the fox, the arctic hare has relatively small ears. If it had larger ears, more skin would be exposed to the harsh environment, and the hare would become cold quickly. Because it has smaller ears, the arctic hare does not lose as much body heat.

The next time you leave your shelter, follow the hare's example and pull your hat over as much of your ears and skin as possible. This way, you will not lose essential body heat.

Just like the arctic fox's fur, the feathers of the snowy owl change color. Young owls and females have brown feathers with spots and stripes. However, when a male owl becomes an adult, its feathers turn white. Because of these colors and patterns, the owls can blend into their surroundings. This helps them hide from predators and surprise rodents and birds when they are hunting.

Snowy owls eat lemmings, rabbits, rodents, other birds, and fish. When food is scarce in the Arctic, the owls head south. However, they always return to the Arctic to lay their eggs.

The eggs of the snowy owl are often hunted by the arctic fox. The snowy owl has many methods of protecting its eggs from the fox's large appetite. The owl builds its nest out of dried grass, so the nest is more difficult to see. The female stays with it all the time. When the male owl returns to the nest with food, it moves very slowly, so as not to draw attention to the nest's location.

This way, the arctic fox is less likely to see the nest and will be less likely to eat the eggs. Now, more of the snowy owl's eggs will hatch. If its nest is found, a snowy owl will defend it fiercely, even against animals that are much larger.

The white feathers of the snowy owl make it difficult to see in the winter.

Walruses use their long, sharp tusks to defend themselves against predators.

Walruses are carnivorous marine mammals much larger than seals. A walrus can weigh more than two thousand pounds and reach nine to twelve feet in length. Walruses have two large tusks that grow from their mouths. The tusks of the walrus help it survive in the Arctic. These very long, sharp tusks help walruses defend themselves against predators such as polar bears and killer whales.

The tusks also help them move around on the ice. A walrus will dig its tusks in, and then pull its huge body across the ice.

Like all other mammals, walruses must breathe air. When they need to take a breath, they come up to the surface of the ocean. They also have air sacs in their necks. By filling up these air sacs, walruses float at the ocean's surface. This allows them to sleep with their heads held up above the surface of the water. They can float in the water and sleep, all at the same time!

Walruses can look very clumsy on land. They use their tusks to haul themselves out of the water onto the ice because they cannot use their flippers. However, they are very quick and graceful in the water. On average, they can swim at a speed of four to six miles per hour. That's much faster than humans can swim!

Did you know that walruses must dive as deep as three hundred feet in the arctic waters to find enough clams to eat? Sometimes they eat as many as six thousand clams in one meal.

It is no surprise that their blubber layer can be as much as six inches thick! Without this thick layer, walruses would not be able to dive as deep into the water in search of the clams they need to survive.

Sea otters are also marine mammals that spend most of their time in the water. Sea otters don't have blubber. Instead, they keep warm in the icy water by trapping air in their fur. The fur is very important for their survival.

Sadly, oil spills from passing ships can damage their fur. They can no longer keep warm air next to their skin, causing the sea otters to freeze. In many instances, people have trapped and cleaned otters that swam through oils spills. Once their fur was restored, the otters were set free.

Sea otters are very smart animals and use things they find in their habitat as tools. To open a clam shell and look for food, they will rest a rock on their chest and hit the shell against the rock. This causes the shell to crack open so they can eat the clam inside.

When they want to sleep, sea otters use pieces of seaweed to tie themselves in place. They prefer to stay in one place, instead of floating around the water.

Sea otters spend most of their time in the water.

Caribou and reindeer travel across the arctic land in search of food.

Reindeer and caribou are animals on the move! In fact, caribou can run within ninety minutes of being born. Although they are called different names depending on where they are, reindeer and caribou are considered the same species.

They are herbivorous, or plant-eating, mammals. In the winter they travel in herds through the Arctic to warmer wooded areas where there is less snow. This way, they can find plants to eat. The reindeer uses its hooves to dig for frozen plants below the snow.

Reindeer and caribou have branched antlers, which are used to protect themselves from predators. Both males and females grow antlers.

For thousands of years, the people of the Arctic have kept herds of reindeer for their meat, their hides, and for transportation. More recently, people have begun keeping more reindeer so they can sell the meat and hides as well. These tamed herds are now taking up more of the land, so many wild reindeer have lost much of their natural habitat.

There are many animals to see in the Arctic. However, there are some animals that you will not see during this winter expedition. These animals hide from the harsh winter weather.

Grizzly bears, for example, sleep heavily through the winter months. This sleeplike state is called hibernation. While hibernating, the grizzly bear lowers its heart rate. This saves valuable energy. The bear will then have more energy to escape predators and find food during the spring, summer, and fall.

Lemmings also hide from the harsh conditions. Lemmings are small, short-legged rodents with small ears and long fur. They live and hide in snow tunnels to protect themselves from the frigid climate. These tunnels also keep them safe from snowy owls, who prey upon the small creatures.

Lemmings can be five to seven inches long. They have dark backs and face stripes. During the winter, lemmings are completely white to help them blend in with the snow. They grow longer front claws in the winter too. They can better dig their snow tunnels using these claws. They also use the claws to locate food under the snow. Lemmings feed on roots, shoots, and grass.

Lemmings usually hide during the winter to avoid the cold.

As you can see, there is a wide variety of life here in the Arctic. Although the landscape may look bare, there are plenty of plants and animals that make this frozen place their home. Although life is harsh, they have figured out how to survive, and even thrive, here.

Your adventure is coming to an end, and it is time to return home. Clean up your shelter, gather up your extra food and water, and prepare to leave the Arctic. Make sure you don't leave any litter behind that would pollute the environment. Don't forget to say good-bye to your guide!

You will miss the amazing animals here. It is hard to choose just one as your favorite! But you have many pictures to show your friends and family at home. These pictures will **verify** that you were really in the Arctic!

You may be looking forward to taking off your hat, mittens, jacket, and snowsuit. Just as the fur or feathers of the arctic fox, snowy owl, lemming, and other animals changes thickness from season to season, you will need to change your clothing when you get back home. Like the caribou, you will probably want to move on to a warmer climate. For your next adventure, you may even think that a tropical island sounds pretty good!

Glossary

conquer *v.* to overcome; to get the better of.

destiny *n.* what becomes of someone or something; your fate or fortune.

expedition *n.* a journey of some special purpose, such as exploration, scientific study, or military purposes.

insulated *adj.* kept from losing electricity, heat, or sound by lining or surrounding something with a material that does not conduct the kind of energy involved.

isolation *n.* a state of being separated from others; of being alone.

navigator *n.* a person in charge of finding the position and course of a ship, aircraft, or expedition.

provisions *n.* a supply of food and drink.

verify *v.* to prove to be true; to confirm.